The
Bible's Answer
to
ADDICTION

ALLEN B. LENTINI

ISBN 978-1-64140-151-7 (paperback)
ISBN 978-1-64140-152-4 (digital)

Christian Faith Publishing, Inc.
832 Park Avenue
Meadville, PA 16335
www.christianfaithpublishing.com

Printed in the United States of America

&

LIFE

In Loving Memory of Simone

Introduction

Addiction has become a plague upon American culture, and we need to attack it head on! The addicts who have turned their lives over the *Lord Jesus Christ,* have not only found deliverance from addiction but also have a great peace and joy in their lives being free from addiction.

This book is for the purpose of bringing the addict from deliverance, to a heavenly destiny, founded upon the *Bible* and faith in *Our Lord Jesus Christ.*

"If the Son shall set you free, you shall be free indeed" (John 8:36).

Reality, Part 1

When it comes to Addiction, we have to ask ourselves, "Do I really want to stop getting High?" This is first and foremost. We can't just look for a time-out" when it comes to our "Addiction," but a new way of life. That search begins with us, with me.

This is, of course, "The Bible's Answer to Addiction." This is a program based upon the Bible and saving faith in our Lord Jesus Christ.

Addiction is an outgrowth of man's fallen nature. We first have to come to the realization that addiction is sin; it's not a disease that I've inflicted upon myself, and it's not something that I can blame on others. It's a sin, and the sooner I can come to that realization, then the easier it will be to bring it before God. If we can come to the understanding that I'm dealing with sin in my life, then we can come to the knowledge of who God is. We can then see that the Lord Jesus Christ came and died on the cross to forgive us of our sins. Not only to forgive us but also to deliver us from our sins. The Christian has brought the sin of Addiction to the foot of the cross and asked our Lord Jesus Christ to not only forgive me of my sins but to also take them from me.

> "If we confess our sins, He is faithful and just to forgive us of our sins and to cleanse us from all unrighteousness" (1 John 1:9, NKJV).

God is faithful and just to forgive us of our sins and to "CLEANSE" us from all unrighteousness. God's desire is to restore back to us our humanity. All that Addiction took from us. Our joy, our peace, our desire for those things outside of our Addiction. The things we can accomplish with our God-given talents are restored at the foot of the cross.

> "Therefore, If anyone is in Christ, he is a new creation; old things have passed away; behold, all things have become new" (2 Corinthians 5:17, NKJV).

We are a new creation, and that work starts from within. New motivations, new desires, a new care for those around us (we begin to see the needs of others and not just taken up with our own needs). We have a different view of the world and the things that happen around us. We have a confidence that God is in control and by His Grace can live out each day to His glory. Not that all of a sudden we are perfect, but that we have an understanding that when we sin, we can bring it to the Lord and be forgiven of that sin and find grace to deal with that sin. We have found in our Lord Jesus Christ the strength, the help, and the enabling to not only battle Addiction but to also overcome it.

> "But thanks be to God, who gives us the victory through our Lord Jesus Christ" (1 Corinthians 15:57,

NKJV). So this is an invitation, as we continue on this trek that we call life, to enjoy reality of having our sins forgiven, finding restoration with God, and being put on a path that has joy and peace. We're still going to have trials and tribulation along the way, but in the end, it will be a life that has profound meaning and purpose in relationship to God and eternity.

What we need to see and understand is Who is JESUS CHRIST? Who is this person that the Christian calls Lord and Savior?

1) He alone is God! He alone can forgive sin.

When Jesus saw their faith, he said to the paralytic, "Son, your sins are forgiven you." (6) But some of the scribes [RELIGIOUS RULERS] were sitting there and reasoning in their hearts, (7) "Why does this Man speak blasphemies like this? Who can forgive sins, but God alone?" (8) But immediately, when Jesus perceived in His spirit that they reasoned thus within themselves, He said to them, "Why do you reason about these things in your hearts? (9) Which is easier, to say to the paralytic, 'Your sins are forgiven,' or to say, 'Arise, take up bed and walk'? (10) But that you may know that the son of Man has power on earth to forgive sins"— He said to the paralytic, (11) "I say to you, arise, take up your bed, and go your way to your house." (12) Immediately he arose..." (Mark 2:5–12)

When you come to the Lord Jesus Christ for forgiveness of sins, you are not coming to a holy man or a good man, but you are coming to God, as the scribes said only God can forgive sins, and that's exactly what our Lord Jesus Christ does. He forgives sins.

2) He came to show us that there is a better way. "The thief does not come except to steal and to kill and to destroy, I have come that they may have life and that they have it more abundantly" (John 10:10, NJKV).This world is nothing more than a death trap, and Addiction is one of the surest ways to know we have fallen into it.

God's desire is that we might have a more abundant life through His Sons Jesus Christ. He wants to take from us those things that destroy us and ultimately end up killing us. It's our Lord's desire to show us the good things that life has to offer

Finally brethren, whatever things are true, whatever things are noble, whatever things are just, whatever things are pure, whatever things are lovely, whatever things are of good report, if there is any virtue and if there is anything praiseworthy-meditate on these things (9c) and the God of peace will be with you. (Philippians 4:8–9, NKJV)

The God of peace will be with you. There are so many good things in this life and in this world that God has given us to enjoy. We don't need to choose those things that will destroy us and lead us to death.

3) He came to die and to give us the ability to live and enjoy that more abundant life
   "And He died for all, that those who live should no longer for themselves, but to Him who died and rose again" (2 Corinthians 5:15, NKJV). "Who died for us that whether we wake or sleep we should live together with Him" (1 Thessalonians 5:10).

That more abundant life is found in Him—just think of it—that He was willing to die to provide for us a life here on earth where we can find complete satisfaction in Him. With that satisfaction also comes a peace that passes understanding.

"And the peace of God, which surpasses all understanding will guard your hearts and minds through Jesus Christ" (Philippians 4:7).

Our Lord's desire for us is good, not evil. All we need to do is simply trust Him so that we might realize all that He has in store for us.

Is Addiction a Sin or a Disease?

"Whatever is not from faith is sin" (Rom 14:23B).

As I pondered this question a few questions came to my mind.

1) While I was active, was I sinning?
2) Is addiction from God or Satan?
3) Does active addiction bring me closer to God?
4) Does addiction lead to eternal life in Our Lord Jesus Christ or Death?
5) If it's a disease, why then does God send people to Hell for it?
   a) The reason why I ask this question is because if Addiction is a Disease, then I can't be held responsible for my actions, because I was simply acting out because of my disease. I was sick and that's why I did the things I did.
   b) As a Christian, we believe that there are two forces in this world that affect the individual and his lifestyle. Now those of us who have viewed addiction have found that it is a destructive force on society. Leaving a wake of

death and sorrow on those who are afflicted by it.

c) If something doesn't bring us closer to God, then it is of the Devil.

You are of your Father the Devil and the "DESIRES" of your father you want to do. He was a "murderer" [ADDICTION KILLS] from the beginning and does not stand in the truth, because there is no truth in Him. When he speaks a lie, he speaks from His own resources, for he is a liar and the father of it. (John 8:44, NKJV)

All that Addiction does to the individual is seen in this verse, itdiverts our desires away from God. Look at the murder and mayhem that addiction bring to a society. And how often do we live in a world full of lies, to ourselves, our families, and our friends. Addiction brings out the worst in the individual.

d) Active Addiction does not bring us closer to Christ which is the only way for a person to attain "Eternal Life."

"And I [Jesus] give them eternal life and they shall never perish" (John 10:28).

What Addiction does is lead us to death.

We see in the verse above that the Devil is a murderer. If something leads us to death and not life, life that is found in our Lord Jesus Christ, then it is Satanic and therefore Sin.

For when you were slaves of sin, you were free in regard to righteousness. (21) What fruit did you have then in the things of which you are now ashamed? For the end of those things is death. (Rom 6:20–21, NKJV)

e) Do you not know that the unrighteous will not inherit the kingdom of God? Do not be deceived. Neither fornicators, nor idolaters, nor adulteres, nor homosexuals, nor sodomites, (10) nor thieves, nor covetousness, nor <u>Drunkards</u>, nor revilers, nor extortioners will inherit the kingdom of Heaven/God. (1 Corinthians 6:9–10)

Now the works of the flesh are evident, which are: adultery, fornication, uncleanness. Licentiousness (20) Idolatry Drug Abuse/ Sorcery, hatred…(21) envy murders, Drunkenness and the like; of which I tell you beforehand, just as I also told you in time past, that those who practice such things will not inherit the kingdom of God. (Galatians 5:19–21)

If Addiction is a disease, then God would be unjust for condemning someone to hell for it. Like all these other sins that are mentioned, these are sins that we human beings choose to do, and they are sins that only by faith in our Lord Jesus Christ can be forgiven.

Addiction comes about for many different reasons in our lives. But when we acknowledge it as sin, then God can deliver us from it.

For a Worldly Perspective, Google/Read:

Dr. Lance Dodes
Is Addiction Really a Disease?
Psychology Today, December 17, 2011

Dr. Marc Lewis's book:
The Biology of Desire: Why Addiction Is Not a Disease
The Clean Slate Addiction Site:
Addiction is "NOT" a brain Disease, it is a choice
Alfred R. Lindesmith, PhD:
Book: Addiction & Opiates

Part 1

Reality of Saving Faith

Satanic Faith

So often when a person begins to get free from Addiction and are in some way brought to a consciousness of God or of a higher power, there seems to be an inclination within their own heart and life to create their own personal God or to become religious, i.e. "I'm going to be a better person." Sadly, this usually ends with a total disregard for the God of the Bible.

It's what I call a "Satanic Faith." This might sound pretty harsh, but let's turn to the Bible to see what it has to say about true genuine saving faith and not that which is concocted by an individual.

> "You believe that there is one God. You do well, even the demons believe and tremble" (James 2:19, NKJV).

We see that demons or fallen angels believe in God. Probably because they have seen Him in His glory before they fell and became demonic. We see in Job 1:6–9:

> Now there was a day when the sons of God (angels) came to present themselves before the Lord, and Satan also came among them (7) and the Lord said

to Satan "From where do you come?" So Satan answered the Lord (God) and said, "From going to and fro on the earth, and from walking back and forth on it," (8) Then the Lord(God) said to Satan, "Have you considered my servant Job that there is none like him on earth, a blameless and upright man, one who fears God and shuns evil?" (9) So Satan answered the Lord (God). (NKJV)

We see that Satan not only believes in God as well, but has also had conversations with God. Now does that mean because Satan believes in God and speak with God, that he is going to heaven? I don't think so.

Now in the synagogue there was a man who had a spirit of an unclean demon, And he cried out with a loud voice, (34) saying "Let us alone! What have we to do with you, Jesus of Nazareth? Did you come to destroy us? I know who You are—the Holy One of God!" (41) And demons also came out of many crying out and saying, "You are the Christ, the son of God!" And He [Jesus], rebuking them, did not allow them to speak, for they knew that He was the Christ. (Luke 4:33–34, 41, NKJV)

The demons knew who Jesus was, and they were terrorized by Him for they knew that He was God, manifested in the flesh who had come to earth. They also submitted to His authority as God. Now obviously the demons believed and knew that Jesus was God, does that mean that they're going to heaven? I don't think so. My point is this, by saying "I BELIEVE IN GOD, SO NOW LEAVE ME ALONE OR MAYBE, *BUZZ OFF*" is actually less of faith in God than that which the demons have.

Religious Faith

We also like to get religious. I think that mankind in general loves religion. Mostly because when we get religious, we feel like we've done something for God. We went to church, we observed a holy day, we didn't eat meat on Friday, I stopped swearing, so on and so forth. Never realizing that God wants our heart and not our actions. If God get ahold of our heart, then our life will change as well. So let's take a look at the religious man in Luke 18:9:

> Also He spoke this parable to some who trusted in themselves that they were righteous, and DESPISED others: (10) Two men went up to the temple to pray, one a Pharisee (RELIGIOUS RULER) and the other a tax collector (11) The Pharisee stood and prayed thus with "Himself," God I thank you that I am not like other men extortioners, unjust, adulterers, or even as this tax collector.(12) I fast twice a week: I give tithes if all that I possess: (13) And the tax collector, standing afar off, would not so much as raise his eyes to heaven, but beat his breast saying "God be merciful to me a sinner!" (14) I tell you, this man went

down to his house justified rather than the other: for everyone who exalts himself will be abased and he who humbles himself will be exalted." (NKJV)

We see the Pharisee, the religious man, and we see that he's very taken up with himself. Five times, we see he says "I": I do this, I do that, aren't I wonderful to God, and I know God is so lucky to have me. The religious man is very taken up with what he is doing for God and not what God has done for him. Unlike the tax collector who acknowledged his sin, to the point where he couldn't even lift his head to heaven. The religious man doesn't even see that he's a sinner in need of a Savior and forgiveness of his sin. But let's move on. If we want to be religious and stand on our good works making us worthy of heaven, then we should know what God's standard is for those who want to do it on their own.

"Therefore you shall be perfect, just as your Father in Heaven is perfect" Matthew 5:48, NKJV). "If we say that we have no sin, we deceive ourselves and the truth is not in us" (1 John 1:8).

God's standard for the religious is sinless perfection. The only problem is that God has told us that if we think we are sinless, then we are really delusional. If you want to be accepted by God through religion, then you need to be perfect. This obviously is unattainable by sinful, fallen mankind.

True Faith

The thing we need in our life to properly deal with Addiction and sin is a proper understanding of true saving faith. That comes first and foremost by building on the understanding of who the Lord Jesus Christ is.

> He said to them, "But who do you say that I am?" (16) Simon Peter answered and said, "You are the Christ, the Son of the living God."(17) Jesus answered and said to him, "Blessed are you Simon Bar Jonah, for flesh and blood has not revealed this to you, but My father who is in heaven. (Matthew 16:15–17, NKJV)

It's of the utmost importance that we get this. Nothing else matters if we don't come to the reality that Jesus is the Christ, the Son of the living God.

> But Jesus answered them: My father has been working until now and I have been working" (18) Therefore the Jews sought all the more to kill Him, because He not only broke the Sabbath, but also said that God was His Father, making Himself equal to God. (John 5:17–18)

We see that Peter acknowledged that Jesus was God, but Jesus's response to Peter was that God the Father had revealed it to him. The thing we need to see is that if I truly want a relationship with God in my life, then creating my own God isn't going to do it, but a heartfelt desire to know Him. I know beyond any shadow of a doubt that God will gladly reveal Himself to whoever comes to Him with that kind of desire.

When I acknowledge that I'm a sinner in need of a savior, God opens his heart to us.

> "For God so loved the world that He gave his only begotten Son, that whoever believes in Him should not perish but have everlasting life" (John 3:16, NKJV).

God so loved us that He opened and made a way of knowing Him thru our Lord Jesus Christ.

> "And this is eternal life, that they may know you the only true God and Jesus Christ whom you sent" (John 17:3, NKJV).

True saving faith is that which acknowledges Jesus Christ as their Lord and Savior, and their worship is directed toward Him

> "But the hour is coming, and now is, when the true worshipers will worship the Father in Spirit and truth; for the Father is seeking such to worship Him" (John 4:23).

Reality What is Man?

"What is man that you are mindful of Him, and the son of man that you visit him" Psalm 8:4, NKJV).

The Psalmist, while contemplating the universe and the glory of God and all that He has done, look upon himself, puny little man in comparison to this vast universe, lifts up his voice almost thinking out loud and states, "What is man that you are mindful of him.

In comparison to the universe, we are nothing, and yet God has put man above all of His creation. Why has man been given such a standing before God? Because we are created in His image. We are the apex, the greatest thing that God created, greater than the whole universe. And so God is mindful of man. Since creation, God's desire for man has always been fellowship, communion, and the relationship of a Heavenly Father with His children.

So let's take a look at this wondrous creation that God calls "MAN.

Then God said, "Let Us make man in Our image, according to Our likeness; let them have dominion over the fish of the sea, over the birds of the air, and over the cattle, over all the earth and over every creeping thing that creeps on the earth." (27) So God created man in His own image; in the image of God He created him; male and female He created them. (Genesis 1:26–27, NKJV)

We are created in the image and likeness of God. No other thing in this universe has been so uniquely created as man. Man was created with the manifold wisdom of the Triune Godhead for we see in verse 26 that God says "Let us" createman. We were created within the counsel of the Father, Son, and Holy Spirit. The creation of man was well thought out. It wasn't simply "Let there be light" (Genesis 1:3), but "Let Us" create man. It's so important to see that man wasn't just an adendumn to creation, but man was the pinnacle of God's creation. God created us for such a glorious plan and purpose, to have a dominion over all of His creation and to have unfettered fellowship and communion with Him.

Now if we were created in His image, then one might ask, "What exactly is the image of God?"

> "This is the message which we have heard from Him and declare to you, that God is light and in Him is no darkness at all" (1 John 1:5, NKJV).

We see that God is light. This is only one of His attributes, and I'll be sharing more as we go along.

> "Who alone has immortality, dwelling in unapproachable light" (1 Timothy 6:16, NKJV).

God not only is light but He also dwells in light, and one day, His light will light the universe.

> And the city has no need of the sun or the moon to shine in it, for the glory of God illuminated it, and the lamb (The Lord Jesus Christ) is it's light. (24) And the nations of those who are saved shall walk in its light. (Revelation

Think of the brilliance and glory of the light of God's glory in that the whole universe is lit and radiates with it.

We also see that God is holy

"But as He who called you is Holy, you also be holy in all your conduct, (16) because it is written, 'Be holy, for I am Holy'" (1 Peter 1:15–16, NKJV). God is also sinless.

> "And you know He was manifest to take away our sins, and in Him there is no sin" (1 John 3:5, NKJV).

> "For He made Him who knew no sin to become sin for us" (2 Corinthians 5:21, NKJV).

God is immortal or eternal

> "Who alone has immortality" (1 Timothy 6:16).

These are but a few of the attributes or characteristic of who God is, but these same traits God gave to man at the time of his creation. God clothed us with His light or glory. God created us to be sinless. He created us to live forever. Think of all the plans and purpose God had for us, for His creation, and for fellowship with Him throughout all of eternity.

Man before the fall had the privilege to know God and enjoy all of His attributes in an experiential way. His love, His holiness, His brilliance, His fellowship without the impediment of sin.

Man at the Fall

So God creates man in all of His glory and all the privilege to enjoy all that God is, but He gave man one stipulation.

> And the Lord God commanded the man, saying, "of every tree of the garden you may freely eat; (17) but of the tree of the knowledge of good and evil you shall not eat, for in the day that you eat of it you shall surely die" (Genesis 2:16–17, NKJV)

So what does man (Adam) do? He eats of the tree of knowledge of good and evil. Now we need to see and understand that EVIL had now entered into the heart of man and the world. By the knowledge of evil, man was now able to commit any sin that his wicked heart could devise. That same heart that enjoyed the love and fellowship of God, that shared in the holiness of God, has now become the most wicked thing on earth.

> "The heart is deceitful above all thing, and desperately wicked; who can know it?" (Jeremiah 17:9, NKJV).

Only God can know the human heart better than even you or I can know it. Not only did "Evil" enter into the world, but by Adam, death also entered into the world.

> "Therefore, just as through one man, sin entered the world, and death through sin, and thus death spread to all men, because all have sinned" (Romans 5:12, NKJV)

Prior to Adam's sin and the fall of mankind, man was created to live forever. When you think of it, wouldn't man/Adam have been better off never knowing evil? What exactly did he gain by understanding and knowing evil? It just like Addiction. If we had never known about a drink or drugs, wouldn't we have been better off? It's the same with Adam. When God told him not to eat of the tree of the knowledge of good and evil, it was for his best. It wasn't to keep Adam from something wonderful. Quite the contrary, it was to keep him from the most horrible thing and things he could ever imagine. It's the same way when someone warns you to stay away from drugs and alcohol. It's not to keep you from something good, but to keep you away from a life of sorrow and remorse that most often leads to death. You have to always, always remember, "God's intentions for you is good." He wants the best for you, just as He did for Adam. The lie we buy as addicts is that Addiction is something wonderful, something that's going to meet our needs and fill that gap of emptiness in our lives. A gap that only the Lord Jesus Christ can fill.

Man at Redemption

So mankind has fallen into sin, and by that sin he is separated from God. But God who loves man being rich in mercy now begins a way back to Himself for fallen, sinful man.

> The Lord is merciful and gracious, slow to anger, and abounding in mercy. (9) He will not always strive with us, nor will He keep his anger forever. (10) He has not dealt with us according to our sins, nor punished us according to our inequities (11) For as the heavens are high above the earth, So great is His mercy toward those who fear Him; (Psalm 103:8–11)

It is the mercy of God toward His creation that has caused Him to not give up on us. God created us for fellowship, but sin has interrupted that fellowship. Now God needs to deal with man's sin and provide a way back for man to Himself.

What God now institutes is an offering or a sacrifice that man can make for his sins to God to be able to restore that fellowship.

So it was, when the days of feasting had run their course, that job would send and sanctify them [His Children] and he would rise early in the morning and offer burnt offerings according to the number of them [His Children] all. For Job said, "It may be that my sons have sinned and cursed God in their hearts." This job did regularly. (Job 1:5, NKJV)

What we see there is that Job as a godly father would offer sin offerings in behalf of his children. But what we see is that there needed to be an offering normally, a lamb, a bull, turtle doves, but there had to be the death and the shedding of the blood of the offering for the forgiveness of sin. This was a signpost that God was showing to mankind leading us to the ultimate sacrifice of God's son our Lord Jesus Christ on the cross.

"Without shedding of blood there is no remission [of Sins]" Hebrews 9:22b, NKJV)

All this might sound a little strange to someone who just came to accept Jesus as their Lord and Savior or to one who is curious about who this Jesus guy is. But what I'm stating is God's way back to Himself. There had to be a sacrifice for sins, and that sacrifice was our Lord Jesus Christ being nailed to the cross and shedding His blood so that we can be forgiven of our sins, and our fellowship restored back to God. God didn't leave it up to us, but He acted in our behalf.

When we put our faith and trust in the Lord Jesus Christ, not only are our sin forgiven, but all that God had intended for us before the fall of man is restored; His plans, His purpose, all that He desired for man is given back to us. Though we might not see it right now as we look at ourselves and wonder what God saw in me that would compel Him to go and die on the cross in my behalf. Yet at the time of salvation, God infuses us with His glory. We might not see it, but those around us so often will say, "Boy, have you changed since you become a Christian." It's God's glory that brings about that change in our lives, and though we might not see it, we can still give God all the credit for the change that He is bringing about in our lives.

> "For our light affliction which is but for a moment, is working, for us a far more exceeding and eternal weight of glory" (2 Corinthians 4:17, NKJV).

To God be the glory for all the things he has already done in our lives, and for all the things He is going to do.

Recognition

"For as a man thinks in his own heart, so is He" (Proverbs 23:7).

How do we view the surpassing greatness of the blessing of being free from drug and alcohol abuse in our lives? Do we see it as a new lease on life or a bummer because I can't get high anymore? Rather than embracing the joy of waking up sober and straight each morning and living each day to its fullest, we become bitter and disgruntled because the fun has been removed from our lives.

> "Why are you disquieted within me? Hope in God; For I shall yet praise Him. The help of my countenance and my God" (Psalms 42:11, NKJV).

We need to see that being free from addiction not only gives us a new direction in our lives, but it also enables us to be restored back to our creator, to our God. To put our hope and trust in Him, Our Lord Jesus Christ.

1) Can I have joy in sobriety and being straight?
   "Being confident of this very thing, that He who has begun a good work in you will complete it until

the day of Jesus Christ" (Philippians 1:6). "For it is God who works in you both to will and to do for His good pleasure" (Philippians 2:13).

By turning our lives over to Jesus Christ, there is a work that God Himself has begun in our lives. But it's the hope that God gives us as He begins that work in our lives. This hope and the understanding that our lives will have meaning and a purpose. Not that we'll just fritter the hours away wondering what we're going to do now that we don't get high. Now it's the expectation to see what God is going to do, to me and thru me.

> "But now, O Lord, you are our Father. We are the clay and you our potter; And all we are the work of your hand" (Isaiah 64:8, NKJV).

God is the potter, and we are the clay. He is molding us into something glorious that will bring glory and honor and praise to Him. It's this expectation to see what God is going to do that should be the motivation of our hearts like it said in Philippians 2:13: "For it is God who works in 'YOU' both to will and to do for 'HIS' good pleasure." What God is doing in our lives is in accordance to His perfect will for our lives. Every incident in our lives throughout the course of the day is an opportunity for us to learn and grow by.

2) What is our expectation?
   Another parable He put forth to them saying: "The Kingdom of Heaven is like a mustard seed, which

> a man took and sowed in his field, (32)" Which
> indeed is the least of all seeds; but when it is grown
> it is greater than the herbs and becomes a tree,
> so that the birds of the air come and nest in its
> branches. (Matthew 13:31–32, NKJV)

Our expectation is that we are a part of something much greater than myself. That my existence isn't solely based on me anymore, but that I am part of something much larger than me. I am now part of God's Kingdom here on earth. I am part of a movement that has eternal ramifications. What do we see about that Kingdom? It's that it begins with something as small and as simple as a mustard seed. It's that work that began in our lives when we put our faith and trust in the Lord Jesus Christ. The thing about having a Kingdom is that you need willing subjects to make up that Kingdom.

> But you are a chosen generation, a royal priesthood,
> a holy nation. God's own special people, that you
> may proclaim the praises of Him who called you
> out of darkness [ADDICTION] and into His mar-
> velous light (10) Who were once not a people but
> are now the people of God. (1 Peter 2:9–10)

We have been called out of this world and the things of this world to become God's special people. We are the ones who now constitute His Kingdom, the Kingdom of God here on earth.

"He has delivered us from the power of darkness (Drugs and Alcohol) and translated us into the Kingdom of the Son of His love," (Colossians 1:13, NKJV) "Who gave Himself for us, that He might redeem us from every lawless deed and purify for Himself His own special people, zealous for good works" (Titus 2:14).

We have been redeemed, we have been purified, so that He can call us His own, those who make up His Kingdom here on earth. We are those who acknowledge Him as our Lord and Master, but also as our King.

"So He said to them, "When you pray, say: Our Father in Heaven Hallowed be your name, Your Kingdom Come" (Luke 11:2a, NKJV).

We see that our prayers are to be for His Kingdom to come to this earth in its fullness. Think also of the millions of Christians that acknowledge Jesus as their King. This is His Kingdom here on earth.

NKJV LK 11:23 "Your will be done on earth as it is in heaven" (Matthew 6:10).

This is why we pray "Thy will be done on earth as it is in heaven." We know that God rules in heaven, but on earth, we need to constantly be in prayer concerning His will to be done in our lives. We're sinners. We need God's help each and every day to do and accomplish His will in our lives.

We also see in Matthew 13:31–2 that the mustard seed grows. The work that God began in our lives as a mustard seed then grows into a tree.

> "As newborn babes, desire the pure milk of the word, that you may grow thereby," (1 Peter 2:2, NKJV). "But grow in the grace and knowledge of our Lord Jesus Christ," (2 Peter 3:18). "But speaking the truth in love, may grow up in all things into Him who is the head—[Our Lord Jesus] Christ" (Ephesians 4:15).

The Christian life is a life of growth. Through the experiences that we encounter throughout our lives. It also comes by being involved with the house of God, His church, because that's where our brethren are and fellow members of the Kingdom of God and heaven.

3) Learn from those who went before us.
   These all died in faith, not having received the promises, but having seen them afar off were assured of them, embraced them, and confessed that they were strangers and pilgrims on earth. (14) For those who say such things declare plainly that they seek a homeland. (15) And truly if they had called to mind that country from which they had come out, they would have had opportunity to return. (16) But now they desire a better….Therefore God is not ashamed to be called their God, for He has prepared a city [Kingdom] for them. (Hebrews 11:13–16, NKJV)

We have become strangers and pilgrims here upon this earth. We're just passing through. Our home is somewhere beyond the blue. God has prepared for us a place in heaven, and throughout this life, He is making us ready for that home, and a place with him through all eternity.

Restoration

Intro

Coming out of a life affected by addiction and the people we associated within those circles, we would naturally have issues with trust. So to be able to turn our life over to the care of someone and entrust Him with our innermost thoughts and desires is somewhat revolting. Mainly because many of us have been taken advantage of or burned by others. When the Bible says in Proverbs 3:5: "Trust in the Lord with all your heart and lean not on your own understanding;" we kind of recoil at the thought because we've had to make our way in this life on our own. I guess the million-dollar question is: "How did that work out for ya?"

Proverbs 3:5 says, "Trust in the Lord with all your heart and lean not on your 'OWN' understanding." The problem we have as individuals, as human beings, is "our" understanding is limited because of who we are. The Lord says in Isaiah 55:8: "'For my thoughts are not your thoughts, nor are your ways my ways,' say the Lord."

Verse 9: "For as the heavens are higher than the earth, so are my ways higher than your ways, And My thoughts than your thoughts." What we have to see is that when we entrust our lives to the Lord Jesus Christ, it's not as if we're entrusting ourselves to a best friend, but To God Himself. to the point that even though I don't understand it all, I can be assured that His ways will always be for my good.

> So let's take a look at a man who was willing to leave all at the call of Our Lord Jesus Christ and follow Him. "As Jesus passed on from there, He saw a man named Matthew sitting at the tax office. And he said to him, 'Follow Me' and he arose and followed Him" (Matthew 9:9). LK 5:27 "After these things He went out and saw a tax collector name Levi, sitting at the tax office. And he said to him, 'Follow Me.' And he left ALL, rose up, and followed Him" (Luke 5:27–28).

Now who was this "Matthew Levi"? Probably his first and middle name. Matthew was a tax collector, easily one of the most despised individuals and professions in the nation of Israel. They viewed tax collectors as sellouts to the nation. They were excommunicated from the temple and all religious gatherings. It wasn't a noble profession because they made the rules as they went along. There was no tax code. The tax code was whatever they wanted to tax. A tax collector was basically a franchise sold to them by the Roman government. They were given an area, and they would extract as much in taxes from that area to be able to make their living. It was a very prosperous way to make a living. In today's money, he would probably be making somewhere between $250,000 to $1,000,000. So like I said, it was very lucrative.

What do we see though when Christ came to Him and said follow me?. He left all and entrusted himself to the Lord 100 percent. When it says he left all, he really did. His mansion, his Wall Street job, his friends—he left all. Once you left your spot as a tax collector, there was someone there to immediately take your place, and you never get it back.

Just a couple of things to notice when the Lord called Matthew. 1) He didn't say, "Follow me, and I'll make you a better person." No. The Lord just said, "Follow me." 2) He didn't say, "Follow me, and I'll make all your troubles go away," or "Follow me and I'll make you rich," or "Follow me, and you'll be happy for the rest of your life." Nope. When the Lord calls us to follow Him, He call us to trust Him and believe that His intentions for us are nothing less than the best for us. But isn't it also exciting that He comes to us with no explanation or hint of what the future holds, but just simply saying, "Follow Me." Notice also that the Bible says in Matthew 9:9: "As Jesus passed on from there, 'HE' saw a man name Matthew sitting at the tax office. And He said to him, 'Follow Me.'" We see that Matthew wasn't running around looking for the Lord, but he was just sitting there, just doing his job at the tax office. And the Lord came to him. Isn't that the way it is in so many of our lives? While we're simply involved in the mundane operation of our day, the Lord comes to us and calls us, "Follow Me." Maybe you thought it or had a discussion with someone. Maybe you just happened to turn on a Christian radio station or someone dragged you out to a Bible study and you heard the call of God in your life. And you determined at that time in your life to forsake all and "Follow Jesus." In my life, I was seventeen, spending a summer in Rockland, Maine, which is eight hours from my home. I just happened to find a book titled *The Late, Great Planet Earth*. I read it, and when I was done, I got on my knees and asked "Jesus" into my life, and that's where the journey began. He came to me when I least expected it, and I responded to that call, and what a journey it's been.

We can trust the Lord with our all. We can turn over everything to the Lord and entrust Him with it. "Our life": "For you died, and your life is hidden with Christ in God" (Colossians 3:3). Our lives are safely hidden away in and with God. "Our weakness": "And He said to me, 'My grace is sufficient for you, for My strength is made perfect in weakness'" (2 Corinthians 12:9).

"Our Addiction": "Therefore, if anyone is in Christ, he is a new creation, old things have passed away, behold all things have become new" (2 Corinthians 5:17). Our addiction is old news, it's a thing of the past. We are now looking forward, it's a new day. "Old things have passed away, behold all things have become new."

"Our Emotional Pain & Agony": "Who forgives all your iniquities, who 'Heals' all your diseases" (Psalms 103:3). "He heals the brokenhearted and binds up their wounds [sorrows]" (Psalms 147:3).

"Our Sin": "As far as the east is from the West, So far has He removed our transgressions sins from us" (Psalms 103:12). "I, even I, am He who blots out your transgressions for My own sake; And I will not remember your sins" (Isaiah 43:25). "I have blotted out, like a thick cloud, your transgressions, and like a cloud, your sins" (Isaiah 44:22).

"Our Future": "Then we who are alive and remain shall be caught up together with them in the clouds to meet the Lord in the air. And thus we shall always be with the Lord" (1 Thessalonians 4:17). Our future will be spent with our Lord Jesus Christ throughout all eternity.

CLOSE: "There is no fear in love, but perfect love cast our fear" (1 John 4:18). We have nothing to fear by turning our lives over to the Lord Jesus Christ. Perfect love was demonstrated at the cross when our Lord went to the cross to die for our sins and to redeem us back to Himself. He not only told us that He loves us, but He also showed us that He loves us. "In this the love of God was manifested toward us, that God has sent His only begotten son into the world, that we might live through Him. In this is love, not that 'we' loved God, but that 'He' loves us and sent His Son to be propitiation, an atoning sacrifice for our sins" (1 John 4:9–10). "But God demonstrates His own love toward us, in that while we were still sinners, Christ died for us" (Romans 5:8).

As I said when Christ comes and calls you, He is calling you to His best. He gave His best in your behalf. So that we can enjoy all that He intends for us

Praise the Lord for all His goodness. "The Lord is good to all, and His tender mercies are over all His work" (Psalms 145:9).

Reliance

As Christians, we talk about relying upon the Lord and hope by saying that that there is some magical spell that will come upon us, and we will be transformed into some kind of super Christian, and life will be just wonderful from that point on. In all actuality, it's really just the opposite. Not that all of a sudden life is going to be miserable and intolerable, but life will change for the person who has put their faith and trust in the Lord Jesus Christ. Our Lord has called us with a very unique calling. In 2 Corinthians 6:17, it says, "Come out from among them and be separate, says the Lord." The Lord has separated us from this world. He has called us out of it. We are now different from the world (i.e., the desires, the pursuit, the thing that those around us think are important). He has called us to Himself and has put us at odds with the world and, in most cases, those around us. You are now a Christian. You call Jesus Christ Lord and those around us look at us as if we're a little odd.

So when I talk about relying upon the Lord, it's not just strength to make it through the day, but also to handle situations that arise throughout the course of our day. It's His enabling to keep us through this life.

So how about some simple principles concerning Reliance upon the Lord.

1) Rely upon Him for your salvation. "Who has saved us and called us with a holy calling, not according to our works, but according to His own purpose and grace which was given to us in Christ Jesus before time began" (2 Timothy 1:9).

When God called you be a Christian, He called you because He had a plan and a purpose for your life. That plan for your life was thought out by God "Before Time Began." God knows what He intends for you. You just need to trust Him for it. "For we are His workmanship, created in Christ Jesus for good works, which God prepared <u>beforehand</u> that we should walk in them" (Ephesians 2:10). "Therefore, if anyone is in Christ, he is a new creation" (2 Corinthians 5:17). "For it is God who works in you both to will and to do for 'His' good pleasure" (Philippians 2:13).

When we rely upon God for our salvation, we see that it's all of Him. We just need to be confident that He knows! What He's doing each and every step of the way.

2) Rely upon Him in our daily living. "The steps of a good man are ordered by the Lord, And 'He' delights in his way. (24) Though he fall, he shall

not be utterly cast down; For the Lord upholds him with His hand" (Psalms 37:23–24). Throughout our day, we might stumble and fall, but it is the Lord who picks us up. All we need to do is brush off the dust and keep walking.

"If you love ME, keep my commandments. (16) And I will pray the Father, and He will give you another HELPER, that He may abide with you forever—(17) the Spirit of truth, whom the world cannot receive, because it neither sees Him nor knows Him; but you know Him, for He dwells with you and will be in you. (18) I will not leave you orphans; I will come to you" (John 14:15–18). As we walk through this life, the Lord hasn't left us to the wolves, but He has provided us with a helper, the Holy Spirit dwelling in us, leading us, keeping us, and strengthening us so that we can make it through each and every day with total reliance upon Him, our Lord Jesus Christ.

3) We can rely upon Him for a future hope. "For I consider that the sufferings of this present time are not worthy to be compared with the glory which shall be revealed in us" (Romans 8:18). "Therefore we do not lose heart. Even though our outward man is perishing, yet the inward man is being renewed day by day. (17) For our light affliction, which is but for a moment, is working for us a far more exceeding and eternal weight of glory, (18) while

we do not look at the things which are seen, but at the things which are not seen. For the thing which are seen are temporary, but the things which are not seen are eternal" (Romans 8:18). That unseen work that God is doing in you. So often I say all I can see in me is a sinner. The longer I walk with the Lord, the more aware I am of just how wretched a sinner I am, yet those around us so often see something totally different than we do. And that's the eternal work of God in our lives. Sure there will be suffering along the way, and there will be growing pains as we become mature adults in our faith, but even with that, we have to see that God's plan for us is a glorious plan. "Eye has not seen, nor ear heard, nor have entered into the heart of man. The things which God has prepared for those who love Him" (1 Corinthians 2:9). We cannot comprehend all that God intends for us throughout all of eternity with Him, all we know is that it's glorious. "Looking for the blessed hope and glorious appearing of our great God and Savior Jesus Christ" (Titus 2:13). We have such a hope and a destiny laid up for us in heaven. When we see that, then the things of this world become less and less important.

Finally, it's a heavenly hope that our Lord has given us, a future provided by Him, and gloriously designed by Him. "In my Father's house are many mansions; if it were not so, I would have told you. I go to prepare a place for you" (John 14:2). "Now I saw a new heaven and a new earth, for the first heaven and the first earth had passed away" (Revelation 21:1). This is God's intention for His own. For those who have put their faith and trust in Him. For those who have turned everything over to Him and have learned the sweet lesson of complete RELIANCE on a Loving, gracious, and merciful HEAVENLY FATHER.

"Removal"

"Therefore, if anyone is in Christ, he is a new creation; old things have passed away; behold all things have become NEW" (2 Corinthians 5:17).

We see that when we accept Jesus Christ as our Lord and Savior that He gives us a new beginning, we are a new creation, we get a fresh start. Now does that mean that all that baggage we used to drag around with us automatically disappears? Unfortunately, the answer to that is no. God has forgiven us, yet we know in so many cases that we have made a complete mess. Whether it be our lives, our families, our finances or whatever else we came in contact with. Now obviously I am not saying this about everyone. Many alcoholics get up and go to work every day and function as alcoholics, but I don't believe that anyone walks away from addiction without any scars.

So how do we deal with the sorrows of our past life and begin our new life in Christ a fresh? Well, I would like to look to the apostle Paul. Prior to coming to Christ, Paul had a past. At that time, he was known as Saul—Saul of Tarsus—and he was a Pharisee, a religious ruler. It was his job to capture and imprison and, in some cases, kill

Christians. "Now Saul was consenting to his [Stephen] death. At that time a great persecution arose against the church which was at Jerusalem; and they [the believers] were all scattered throughout the regions of Judea and Samaria, except the apostles" (Act 8:1). "As for Saul, he made havoc of the church, entering every house, and dragging off men and women, committing them to prison" (verse 3). "Then Saul, still breathing threats and murder against the disciples of the Lord, went to the high priest and asked letters from him to the synagogues of Damascus, so that if he found any who were of the way, whether men or women, he might bring them bound to Jerusalem" (Acts 9:1–2).

Paul viciously persecuted the Church. As a Pharisee, he did it as religious service to God. But once he became a Christian, he had to come to the realization that those who he had locked up in prison and murdered were now his brothers and sisters in Christ. This is a realization that Paul had to deal with for the rest of his life, for we see in 1 Corinthians 15:9: "For I am the least of the apostles, who am not worthy to be called an apostle, because I persecuted the Church of God." "For you have heard of my former conduct in Judaism, how I persecuted the church of God beyond measure and tried to destroy it" (Galatians 1:13)

Paul had a past, and it was something that he had to deal with as a new Christian. So do we. As those who have dealt with addiction in our own lives and the wake of destruction it leaves in our past, we can learn much from the apostle Paul in how he was able to know he was forgiven and to get on with his life in Christ as a new creation in Christ.

1) We have to know we're forgiven. We are forgiven of all of our sins. In many cases we have to seek the Lord to help us clean up the mess we made, for there are still consequences because of our sin and the decisions that we had made. But above all, our sins are "<u>FORGIVEN</u>." When we came to Jesus and accepted Him as our Lord and Savior and we confessed that we are sinners in need of a Savior, at that moment, our "<u>SINS</u>" were forgiven. It was there that God put us on a new path with a new destiny. A new future laid out for us by God Himself. As it said in 2 Corinthians 5:17: "Behold, '<u>ALL</u>' thing have become new." New desires, new goals, a new outlook on life, a newfound joy knowing the Lord is able to accomplish all things in my life if I will simply trust Him.

2) We have to move forward. "Brethren, I do not count myself to have apprehended; but one thing I do, FORGETTING those things which are behind and reaching forward to those things which are ahead" (Philippians 3:13).

We cannot be plagued or continually dragged down by our past. Acknowledge, boy, did I mess things up, but now it's time to start moving forward in our new life in Christ. We need to understand that God has a plan and purpose for our life, as with

Paul. He used that sorrow to motivate him to a life of service and dedication to the Lord. "But by the grace of God I am what I am, and His grace toward me was not in vain; but I labored more abundantly than they all, yet not I, but the grace of God which was with me" (1 Corinthians 15:10).

When Paul says "he labored more abundantly than they all," he was referring to the other apostles. He preached more, he wrote more, and he traveled more. Of the twelve apostles, Paul became the most distinguished apostle throughout the centuries of Christendom, apart from our Lord Jesus Christ. Paul has been the most admired. He stands as a giant amongst those who are mentioned in the Bible. Paul didn't allow his sorrow or guilt to drag him down, but it compelled him to service and an amazing life as a new creation in the Lord Jesus Christ.

I think this gives the new believer such hope and aspiration to know that God can use me as well. I too should be motivated by my past. God can take someone like me and use me to His glory. That, that which I do here on earth can redound through all eternity. God has called us with an amazing calling and has given us an amazing future. We just need to shake off the shackles that would hold us back.

3) We need to learn to serve. We believe that God has called us to something greater than "Woe is me." Believe it or not, service begins with a proper attitude and love for oneself. "If you really fulfill the royal law according to the scripture, 'you shall love you neighbor as you love yourself,' you do well;" (James 2:8). You cannot love you neighbor if you are full of self-loathing and negativity toward yourself. How can you tell others of God's love for them if you haven't allowed God's love to permeate your heart and life? If God saw such great worth in you that He was willing to be nailed to a cross and shed His blood and die for you, then you to need to see what value you have in your own eyes. When you see your own value and worth, then you can see the value and worth there is in others. It becomes much easier to share the Gospel with others when you have that perspective toward your fellow man. To simply start, the most important thing a new Christian can do is join a good Bible-believing church. In the house of God is the greatest place for the young Christian to grow. Thru the Bible study, the prayer meeting Sunday worship, and the friendships you develop with those who love the Lord Jesus Christ as well. Our life in Christ begins with us. Then from there, it branches out to others.

To close, Paul could say at the end of his life in 2 Timothy 1:3: "I thank God, whom I serve with a pure conscience." Even though Paul had to deal with the sorrows and guilt of his persecution of the church, yet when he came to the end of his life, he could say that he served God with a pure conscience. God had put the past behind him. He knew without a doubt and with full assurance that he had truly been forgiven.

Philippians 4:9 (Paul Speaking): "The things which you learned and received and heard and saw in me, these do, and the God of peace will be with you."

AMEN.

Re-Evaluate, Part 1

This chapter is about the things we need to be concerned about as we go forward in our Christian life free from addiction. The things that would distract us and draw us back into a life of addiction and despair. Can I hang out with those that I used to drink and do drugs with? "NO." If you lie down with dogs, then don't be surprised if you wake up with fleas. If you hang out with those that you used to drink and do drugs with, then don't be surprised if you go back to drinking or drugs or both. There has to be a breaking away from those people and things that led you into that destructive behavior. You might say I have no other friends. Not to worry. There are over three hundred million people living in the United States and 80% say that they are Christian, so there are lots of people to choose from. All you need to do is find a good church. It may take a couple of tries but don't get discouraged, our God is a faithful God, and he will lead you to a church that will meet your needs as a Christian.

As a Christian, one of the greatest battles we face in our life each and every day is the draw and influence of the world in our lives.

Do not love the world or the things in the world. If anyone loves the world, the love of the Father is not in him. 16) for all that is in the world-the lust of the flesh, the lust of the eyes, and the pride of life-is not of the Father but is of the world. (17) And the world is passing away, and the lust of it; but he who does the will of God abides forever. (1 John 2:15–17)

What does it mean when the Bible say "LOVE NOT THE WORLD"? Am I now supposed to hate trees, oceans, lakes? A setting sun, sunrise? Of course not. God has declared His glory thru all these things. "The heavens declare the glory of God" (Psalms 9:1). God has given us all these things to enjoy and to express our gratitude and joy to such an amazing Creator.

When the Bible says "Love not the world," this deals with our affections, what we are drawn to, and what entices us. The Bible gives us an example of this in 2 Timothy 4:10: "For Demas has forsaken me having loved this present world." Demas is a man in scripture that I look upon as only second to Judas Iscariot, the man who forsook the Lord. Demas was a companion of the apostle Paul on his missionary journeys as we see in Philemon 1:23–24: "Epaphras, my fellow prisoners in Christ Jesus, greets you, as do Mark, Aristarchus, 'DEMAS,' Luke, my fellow laborers"; "Luke the beloved physician and 'Demas' greet you" (Colossians 4:14). What was it about the world that would draw Demas away from the apostle Paul? Surely he saw the miracles that God performed thru the apostle Paul. He saw the great number of people who came to saving faith in our Lord Jesus Christ, and yet with all of this that he had witness thru the life and ministry of the apostle Paul, the pull and draw, and the things of the world was enough to separate him from Paul. Look again at the witness of the life of the apostle Paul. "Truly the signs of an apostle were accomplish among you with all perseverance, in signs and wonders and mighty deeds" (2 Corinthians 12:12). Demas witnessed all of these and still said, I want the things of this world more than I want the things of Jesus Christ.

What possibly were some of the reasons he decided to forsake Paul and go back and pursue the things of the World?

1) Maybe he didn't like being ostracized. There is a cost to becoming a Christian. You become "one of those"—those "BORN-AGAIN TYPES." There is a certain reproach we bear as those who are followers of Jesus Christ. The world hates our Lord which was demonstrated when they nailed Him to the cross. The masses cried out "CRUCIFY HIM" (Luke 23:21). So if the world hated our Lord, should we be surprised if they hate us as well? It's not easy when you see that your friends and family begin to pull away because you have less and less in common as you pursue your life in Christ. I Peter 4:3,4 "For adequate has been the time that is now past and done with, for you to have carried to its ultimate conclusion the counsel of the pagans (The Unsaved), conducting

yourselves as you have done in disgusting sensualities, in cravings, in wine gaggling's, in carousals, in drinking bouts, and in unlawful idolatries, in which they think it a thing alien to you that you do not run in a troop, like a band of revelers with them in the same slough of dissoluteness, speaking evil of you. "<u>WUEST</u>. They now make fun of you because you don't want to go out and party anymore. If we were to be honest, with most of our friends and acquaintances, the only thing we had in common was partying and not much more. Our Lord has called us to something far greater and more glorious than just partying. But for some, family and friends, they are everything to them, and anything that might come in between those relationships cannot be tolerated.

2) Maybe he said it just isn't worth it. The persecution, the animosity from others, a life based solely on faith and trusting God, rather than having the security of a forty hours a week job, a home to come home to every night, the creature comforts of life. A life of faith and trusting the Lord isn't always easy. Yet when we come to the point in our life that we can trust the Lord for everything, we have a great peace in this life that only comes from the Lord. Demas was shortsighted. He came to a point in his life where he could only see the here and now. He lost sight that he was living his life in light of eternity. God has called us to eternal life. "And I give them eternal life, and they shall never

perish" (John 10:28). We will have all eternity to rest. This life is here today and gone tomorrow in James 4:14: "For what is your life? It is even a vapor that appears for a little while and then vanishes away." What we need to see is that our time here on earth, when you line it up with eternity, is a blink of an eye. Yet what we do with this life will determine our eternity. We can't be shortsighted in the decisions we make or the pursuits we engage in. God didn't call us to be His own so that He can punish us and make our lives miserable. He called us so that He can show us how much He loves us, and by learning to trust Him, we will grow to love Him as our Heavenly Father. God loved Demas, he simply lost sight of that reality.

3) Maybe he thought he was going to get rich laboring with Paul for the Lord. Maybe he allowed himself to have false expectations in following the Lord. Sadly, there are many false preachers today who preach that God is some kind of a get-rich scheme. That if you accept Jesus, He will meet all your needs as <u>you </u>determine them to be. <u>"NO."</u> We don't know what God's plan is for our life. All we can be assured of is that it's the best possible plan for our lives, for it is God who has made those plans in our behalf. That's the joy and the expectation of a life of faith when we commit our life to the Lord. "This is the day the Lord has made" (Psalm 118:24). We believe every day is a creation

of the Lord. Not just a sunrise and a sunset, but everything that comes our way throughout the course of the day. It's a day of blessing and instruction from the Lord. All Demas saw was the struggle and struggles of each day. He lost sight of Paul's example. "For I have learned in whatever state I am, to be content (12) I know how to be abased, and I know how to abound. Everywhere and in all things I have learned both to be full and to be hungry, both to abound and to suffer need. (13) I can do all things through Christ who strengthens me" (Philippians 4:11b–13). I think Demas lost sight of the fact that we live this life in light of God's perfect plan thru this life and all eternity.

When we become Christians, we first need to evaluate the cost of becoming a Christian. This life might not be what we planned for it to be, but guess what? Eternity will be so much more than we ever dreamed it could be. "Eye has not seen, nor ear heard, Nor have entered into the heart of man, The things which God has prepared for those who love Him" (1 Corinthians 2:9).

By forsaking Paul and going back to the world, Demas missed out, by far, the best this life had to offer. While God was in control and preparing him for eternity with Himself. Don't let the draw of this world in your own life cause you to miss out on all that God intends for you.

Re-Evaluate, Part 2

The Battle Within

Do not love the World or the things in the world. If anyone loves the world, the love of the Father is not in him. (16) For all that is in the world-the lust of the flesh, the lust of the eyes, and the pride of life-is not of the Father but is of the world. (17) And the world is passing away, and the lust of it; but he who does the will of God abides forever. (1 John 2:15–17)

The battle with the world is seen in two ways:

1) An internal battle
2) An external battle

What we see in these verses are:

A) The Lust of the Flesh (Passions, desires)
B) The Lust of the Eyes (I want)
C) The Pride of life (Look at Me)

> "Beloved, I beg you as sojourners and pilgrims abstain from fleshly lust which wage war against the Soul" (1 Peter 2:11).

The battle for you, the person, is the battle for your soul, who you are, what you want, who and what you do and love. When our Lord was here on earth, He warned His disciples in Matthew 10:28: "Do not fear those who kill the body but cannot kill the soul. But rather fear Him who is able to destroy both soul and body in hell."

This is the battle that the Christian is engaged in. When our Lord says "love not the world," He is speaking of those things that would draw us away from Him. The desires and wants of our old nature, those things that we, along with the world think are important. Yet all they do is lead us down a path to destruction. So how does the Christian deal with these desires and wants? By simply turning it over to the Lord. In Psalm 24:7–10, it states, "Lift up your heads, O you gate, and be lifted up, you everlasting doors; And the King of Glory shall come in. Who is this king of Glory? The Lord of host, He is the king of Glory." These are the gates to our soul, our senses: 1) Sight, 2) Smell, 3) Taste, 4) Hearing, 5) Touch—the things that affect the inner being of a man. The Lord is saying, open the gates of your soul so that I can come in and flood your soul with My glory. So that our Lord can give us new desires and a new outlook on this life and the world that we live in. We need only to open the gates of our soul, to simply ask Him into our life. Then as the Psalmist says, "He is the Lord mighty in battle." The battle is the Lord's and the victory is the Lord's. We need to only be willing to turn those desires and ambitions over to the Lord. "For if there is first a willing mind, it is accepted according to what one has, and not according to what he does not have" (2 Corinthians 8:12). God see the desires of our hearts. When we've come to that point in our lives where we say "enough," I can't do it anymore on my own, Oh, Lord, I surrender. You come and fight the battles of this life in my behalf. Then the King of Glory will come in, the Lord mighty in battle. Mighty in battle for you. True deliverance not only comes from freedom from addiction but also freedom from sin as well. Freedom to walk and live this life to the Glory of God.

Now it's important to be aware of these things that wage war against our soul.

1) "The Lust of the Flesh""I say then; Walk in the Spirit and you shall not fulfill the lust of the flesh. (17) for the flesh wars against the Spirit and the Spirit against the flesh;....Now the works of the flesh are evident, which are; adultery, sexual immorality, uncleanness, licentiousness, idolatry, sorcery (Drug Abuse), hatred, contentions, jealousies, outburst of anger, selfish ambitions, dissensions, heresies, (21) envy, murder, drunkenness, revelries and the like;" (Galatians 5:16–17, 19–21). God's word has given us the ability to know when we're going astray, when we're submitting to the flesh and deeds of the flesh. The best way to know how not to enter into sin is to know what are the enemies of our soul. By knowing and understanding the flesh, we can then submit ourselves to the Spirit of God and gain the victory over the flesh.

2) "The lust of the Eyes"

Our Lord says in Matthew 5:28: "But I say to you that whoever 'looks' at a woman to lust for her has already committed adultery with her in his heart." God wants to give us purity of heart with those that we deal with around us. To be able to look at the opposite sex, not in a lustful way, but as someone who Christ died for. This is not to diminish the normal God-given attraction that single men and women have for each other. But that attraction won't be based on lust, but a desire to honor the Lord.

3) "The Pride of Life"

This is "Look at me, look at all that I've accumulated, my house, my Car, the hot wife, look at all I've accomplish, and I want more, more stuff." And with all that stuff, you will find that there is no satisfaction in things. The only way to find satisfaction and fulfillment in this life is through faith in Our Lord Jesus Christ. In Ecclesiastes 3:11, it states, "He has put eternity in their hearts." This is why things can never satisfy that gaping hole of eternity in our lives. That can only be filled by the eternal God. The reason why God put eternity in our hearts is, first, to show us that God created us for eternity. That's why we find death to be abnormal to the human existence. And why that gap can only be satisfied by God. It's a very empty life when we put or faith and trust in things and people. Satisfaction comes from above and not the things of this world.

This might sound like a heavy discussion, but it's important to know what we have to deal with as Christians. The best way to know the battle is to know the enemy, and most often the enemy is the enemy within. The old man, the flesh, the enemy of our souls.

It's hard enough to make that decision that I'm going to give up drugs or alcohol or both and live my life straight and sober. But then we have to begin with those internal issues that every human being has to deal with. So this is a chapter to not only help you recognize those battles you have to engage in but also to come out on the other side victorious. We're human beings. Whether addicts or angel, we both deal with the same issues.

It's the inner man that God does His greatest work in our lives. It's the transformation of the person, by the power of the Holy Spirit, that brings glory and honor to our Lord Jesus Christ. In Ephesians 2:10, "For we are His workmanship"; and Philippians 2:13, "For it is God who works in you both to will and to do for His good pleasure." The greatest thing to know as a Christian is that God has taken over the reign of our life. No matter what we are confronted with, we can trust that He is in control of the situation for He alone is God and in that we can rest. He knows our strengths and our weaknesses and wants to use both to His glory. By putting our faith and trust in the Lord Jesus Christ, by opening those gates of our soul to the King of Glory, He has given us such a future in this life to enjoy at His side.

Re-Evaluate, Part 3

The Battle With-Out

"We know that we are of God and the whole world is under the power of the evil one" (1 John 5:19).

The second battle the Christian has to deal with is the world around us. People, places, and things. This is why I ask in "Re-Evaluate," "Can I continue to hang out with those that I used to drink and do drugs with?" "But even if our gospel is veiled, it is veiled to those who are perishing, whose minds the god this age has blinded" (2 Corinthians 4:3–4). The thing we have to ask is, are those people going to help me along with my walk with the Lord or are they going to hinder my desire to walk with the Lord? Just because you quit drinking and/or drugging, it doesn't mean they have. Just because you've turned your life over to the Lord Jesus Christ doesn't mean they're going to. So you have to reevaluate those relationships. The most important thing for you to do at this point is to maintain your fellowship and walk with the Lord. If you guard that, you will maintain your freedom from addiction. "For we have spent enough of our past in doing the will of gentiles, having pursued a course of sensuality, lust, drunkenness, carousals drinking parties.

(4) And in all this "They" (Your Friends) are surprised that you do not run with them into the same excess of dissipation, speaking evil of you" (1 Peter 4:3–4). It's your old friends that are going to say, "Come on, lighten up, you're not fun anymore." Or maybe, "You can drink and still be a Christian." They're really not looking out for your best interest, but instead just want you to go along with the crowd. This is but one of the outside influences that you have to deal with. But there are other influences that we have to deal with from the world. Outside of the body.

The first is False Religion.

The second is Oppressive, tyrannical government

As we see in 1 John 5:19: "The whole world is under the power of the evil one (SATAN)."

This world belongs to Satan, but the believers belong to God. Though we live in the world, we are not to be like the world. We are to be different. We are representatives of Jesus Christ. We are called by His Name, Christians. As Christians, we are to stand out in this world by the difference Jesus has made in our lives. We can't tell our old friends of the glorious salvation that can be found in our Lord Jesus Christ if we are acting just like them. What difference has Christ made in our lives if there's no difference between us and them?

Next we've made a commitment to the Lord and now we want to find a church to fellowship at. But there's so many different denominations how do I figure out what's right biblically. This is where it's important to do a little research and investigating. The reason being is that Satan

(The Devil) is the King of false religion. If he can't keep you from becoming a Christian, then he'll do everything he can to lead you astray as a Christian.

"For such are false apostles, deceitful workers, transforming themselves into apostles of Christ. And no wonder! For Satan himself transforms himself into an angel of light. Therefore, it is no great thing if his ministers also transform themselves into ministers of righteousness, whose end will be according to their works" (2 Corinthians 11:13–15). False teachers look and sound great, but they have one purpose, and that is to lead you astray. It's important to find first and foremost a church that believes that Jesus is the eternal God that became a man, He never became a God, He always was God, and secondly that they believe the Bible is God's word from Genesis to Revelation. That it was written by God for us, His people. Also listen to that still small voice, some might call it your gut, but ask God for His guidance and not what necessarily appeals to you, but what honors the Lord.

Secondly, Oppressive, tyrannical government.

Think how many Christians have been murdered throughout the centuries by oppressive governments. Communism alone is believed to have killed in excess of fifty million Christians. More than the first 1900 years before its inception. Christians are presently being persecuted throughout the Middle East, and it's believed that over two million have been murdered. Over a million were murdered by the Turkish government between 1915–1920, 1.5 million is the estimate. Satan has always used governments to persecute Christians along with false religions, who have killed Christians in the name of the Lord. The point that I am getting at is that to become a Christian is going to cost you something according to this world's standards, but according to God's standard, you will inherit everything. Life is short and passing. Whatever you give up for God in this life will surely be recompensed in the life to come with Him.

"If the world hates you, you know that it hated 'ME' before it hated you. If you were of the world, the world would love its own. Yet because you are not of the world, but 'I' chose you out of the world, therefore the world hates you" (John 15:18–19). We have to remember that there is an animosity toward us from the world. Does that mean we have to walk around looking over our shoulders? Live a life of severe paranoia? Absolutely not! We need to know God is in control. God rules in the affairs of mankind. Satan and the world cannot touch us without Our Lord's permission. The Lord is our protector and defender, "but let all those rejoice who put their trust in You; Let them even shout for joy, because you defend them" (Psalms 5:11). "What then shall we say to these things? If God is for us, who can be against us?" (Romans 8:31). We are the Lord's, and as His Own, He will watch over us. Daily I am grateful that I can commit my day to Him. I can take my hands off the day ahead and leave the rest to His divine will. That in itself keeps me from making a mess of things.

God has given us the privilege to represent Him while here on earth in this life which He has given us. The apostle

Paul stated in Ephesians 6:20: "For which I am an ambassador." Paul saw that this life was far more than just getting up and going to work every day.

More than going to church on Sunday. But that while we're here on earth, as we respond to the call of God in our lives, we are then sent forth to not only represent Him but also His Kingdom here on earth. As many have said in the Lord's prayer: "Thy Kingdom come." We are the prelude to that. The earth is not our home. We're just passing thru on our way to His Glorious Kingdom. That's why no matter how hard the world, people, old friends, people we go to work with every day, no matter how hard they try to get us off track, if we will just stay focused on our Lord and Savior, we will overcome these obstacles and have a very victorious life. Over drugs, alcohol, sex, gambling, over whatever sin it is that would keep us down. We will get the victory. To the one who is victorious, he shall inherit all things, and I will be his God and he shall be My son (Revelation 21:7).

Revelation

"And as it is appointed for men to die once, but after this the judgement" (Hebrews 9:27).

I'm sure some would say, "Wow, what a revelation. You mean we're all going to die? Go figure." Yes, but here's the revelation. Our Lord Jesus Christ has removed from us the fear of death. "In as much then as the children have partaken of flesh and blood, He [Our Lord] Himself likewise shared in the same, that through death 'He' might destroy him [SATAN] who had the power of death, that is, the devil, and release those who through fear of death were all there lifetime subject to bondage" (Hebrews 2:14–15). God in His great mercy and love that He has for us has delivered us from the fear and terror of death. Paul could say in Philippians 1:21: "For me to live is Christ, and to die is gain." Paul's life was dedicated to serving the Lord. He walked with the Lord Jesus Christ day by day and was devoted to Him. All death meant to the apostle Paul was that rather than going home to his house, he just simply went home to be with the Lord in His glorious house.

Our life on earth isn't just a life of service, but it is also developing a friendship and love for the Lord. We know that He loved us because He proved it by dying on a cross for us. "But God demonstrates His own love toward us, in that while we were still sinners, Christ die for us" (Romans 5:8). Yet the change in our lives is that we not only learn to trust the Lord but also to love the Lord. "You shall love the Lord your God with all your heart, with all your soul, and with all you might" (Mark 12:30). This type of love doesn't come overnight. It's a love that grows. Notice the verse says "all" your heart, "all" your soul, "all" you might.

This is a love that grows through a relationship with our Lord. As we entrust our life and our time and our will to the Lord, we then see that He is faithful with that trust. We notice a change in our lives (always for the good) and a change in our circumstances (lived by faith). We begin to seek His will and talk to Him through a daily, if not hourly prayer life. Again as Paul says in 1 Thessalonians 5:17: "Pray without ceasing." As the hymn writer wrote "as He walks with me and He talks with me and He tells me I am His own, and the joy we share as we tarry there, none other, has ever known." Think of it! The Lord God, creator of heaven and earth, takes time for YOU. To listen to your prayer, your concerns, the things that are on your heart. And he brings comfort, security, wisdom and direction, and an undisputed sense of His love for me and the life that I live. By this understanding, it becomes easier and easier to love Him with all my heart, all my soul, and with all my might.

So how should we live out our life for the days the Lord has given us here on earth?

1) "See then that you walk carefully, not as fools but as wise redeeming the time because the days are evil. (17) Therefore do not be unwise but understand what the will of the Lord is. (18) And do not be drunk with wine in which is dissipation; but be filled with the Holy Spirit, (19) speaking to one another in psalms and hymns and spiritual songs, singing and making melody in your hearts to the Lord, giving thanks always for all things to God the Father in the name of our Lord Jesus Christ" (Ephesians 5:15–20). Notice the joy the Lord wants us to have in this life. Warning us to walk wisely and maintain a godly behavior, but also to enjoy our brothers and sisters in Christ. Enjoy the house of God and His people. This life isn't supposed to be miserable, but it's to be characterized by joy, singing, making melody in our hearts, giving thanks. Think how miserable the world is around us and to know we can have true joy and thanksgiving in our lives. It changes the way we wake up and face each and every day.

2) Understand that this life means something. "As it is appointed for men to die once, but after this judgement" (Hebrews 9:27). I think that all people have an innate feeling that this life and how we live it will have consequences. That's why God gave us a

conscience, so that we know right from wrong, and we do that which is right so that we don't suffer the consequences. That's why we have courts, so that a penalty can be given out for wrongdoing or crime. Even so for the Christians. "For we must all appear before the judgement seat of 'Christ,' that each one may receive the things done in the body, according to what he has done, whether good or bad" (2 Corinthians 5:10). There is a day of reckoning coming. But look at who the judge is, the one who we love with all our heart, all our soul, and all our might. It is He who saved us so that we might stand before Him blameless. "Who will also confirm you to the end, that you may be blameless in the day of our Lord Jesus Christ" (1 Corinthians 1:8). This is why He saved us, so that we can be trophies of His grace. So that when we stand before Him, it will bring Him glory for the marvelous work of redemption that He alone did in our lives. As we walk with Him day by day, He removes all fear, not only of death but also the judgement to follow.

3) Our Hope

"Beloved, now we are children of God; and it has not yet been revealed, what we shall be, but we know that when He is revealed, we shall be like Him, for we shall see Him as He is. (3) And everyone who has this hope in Him purifies himself, just as He is pure" (1 John 3:2–3). Today as we live out our days here on earth, we walk by faith. We know that Jesus lives in our heart because He's taken up residence there and has made His presence known by the power of His Holy Spirit. But there is coming a day when we shall see Him, our faith will be sight. We shall also put off these mortal bodies with all its ache and pains and put on immortality.

"For this corruptible must put on incorruption, and this mortal must put on immortality" (1 Corinthians 15:53). God is going to give us a body and the ability to live throughout all of eternity. An eternity where there is no sorrow, no death, no sin, but an existence where we are free to worship the Lord in the beauty of holiness. We have so much to look forward to as Christians. The main thing is that we can't get distracted and lose sight of the goal. Keep all that God intends for us ever before us. As Paul said in Acts 26:19: "Therefore, King Agrippa, I was not disobedient to the heavenly vision." Paul was motivated throughout his life by the heavenly vision of knowing how valuable this life is in regards to eternity. That ultimately this life has great meaning and purpose for the Christian. May we strive to live each and every day with that goal before us. The goal of pleasing our Lord and Savior. The goal of bringing Him glory at the judgement seat of Christ. And lastly, the goal of seeing and being with Him throughout all eternity.

Has God not given us a great life, being free from addiction, and the ability to walk with Him while here on earth day by day?

God Bless.

Allen B Lentini

CPSIA information can be obtained
at www.ICGtesting.com
Printed in the USA
FFOW02n1548180418
46261854-47689FF